D1106490

The Crusaders

By Walter Buehr

G. P. Putnam's Sons
New York

Also by Walter Buehr

KNIGHTS AND CASTLES AND FEUDAL LIFE
THROUGH THE LOCKS: CANALS TODAY AND YESTERDAY
TREASURE: THE STORY OF MONEY AND ITS SAFEGUARDING
HARBORS AND CARGOES
SHIPS OF THE GREAT LAKES
TRUCKS AND TRUCKING
RAILROADS TODAY AND YESTERDAY
CARGOES IN THE SKY
SENDING THE WORD: THE STORY OF COMMUNICATIONS
THE GENIE AND THE WORD: ELECTRICITY AND COMMUNICATION
KEEPING TIME
THE STORY OF THE WHEEL
THE WORLD OF MARCO POLO
THE FRENCH EXPLORERS IN AMERICA
THE SPANISH ARMADA
THE SPANISH CONQUISTADORES IN NORTH AMERICA
CHIVALRY AND THE MAILED KNIGHT
WESTWARD – WITH AMERICAN EXPLORERS

Library of Congress Catalog Card Number: 59-7170
Fifth Impression
MANUFACTURED IN THE UNITED STATES OF AMERICA
08212

Contents

The Leaders

POPE URBAN II – Successor to Pope Gregory VII. Spiritual leader of the crusaders.

ADHEMAR – Bishop of Le Puy. First crusader to take the cross.

PETER THE HERMIT – A wandering monk. Led the first column of crusaders.

BOHEMOND – Son of the Prince of Taranto, Italy. A military leader commanding the knights of southern Italy.

RAYMOND – Count of Toulouse, France. Friend of Adhemar. Military leader of French knights.

GODFREY – Godfrey of Bouillon, Duke of Lower Lorraine, Germany. Military leader in the capture of Jerusalem.

HUGH – Count of Vermandois. Military commander of French knights.

ROBERT – Duke of Normandy. Commander of French Norman knights.

ROBERT – Count of Flanders. Cousin of Robert, Duke of Normandy.

STEPHEN – Count of Blois. Brother-in-law of Robert, Duke of Normandy.

ALEXIUS – Emperor of Byzantium, the Christian Empire of the East.

PETER BARTHOLOMEW – A servant boy who had a vision at Antioch.

KILIJ ARSLAN – Turkish sultan. The Red Lion.

YAGI-SIAN – Turkish governor of Antioch.

IFTIKHAR – Egyptian governor of Jerusalem.

STEPHEN – Shepherd boy who led the French children on the Children's Crusade.

NICHOLAS – Peasant boy who led the German children on the Children's Crusade.

A Call to Arms

In autumn of the year 1095, in south central France, a crowd of nearly two thousand stood in silence to hear the words of one of the greatest men of the day. The words were to inspire one of the strangest movements in history – the crusades. The Christians of Europe were about to begin an incredible series of journeys to the holy city of Jerusalem to try to free it from the hands of the Turks.

The man who uttered the inspiring words was Pope Urban II. In the crowd that heard the Pope speak were two hundred and fifty bishops, four hundred abbots, feudal lords, knights, and hundreds of common people. The message these people heard would spread to the farthest corners of Europe.

Pope Urban II had traveled from Rome, the capital of the Holy Roman Empire, across the Alps into south central France. Months before, he had spread the news through Italy and France, Germany and England, that a council would be held and that he, the Pope, would personally attend. He had kept secret the purpose of his journey. On November 18, 1095, the crowd silently waited in a field east of the town of Clermont.

The Pope, a tall and strong man of middle age, hair and beard a golden color, faced the multitude. Ready now to reveal his secret, he spoke:

"To you these words are spoken, and by you the message will be passed on. Grievous cause has brought me here. From Jerusalem and Constantinople ominous news has come to my ears."

And in the quiet which followed, Pope Urban told the shocked audience that the fierce Turks of Asia Minor had invaded Christian-held lands around Constantinople and now held the holy city of Jerusalem.

"The barbarous Turks have torn down the houses of God everywhere," the Pope continued. "They befoul the altars and use the churches as stables.

"They have led away into slavery many Christian pilgrims to the Holy Land. Those pilgrims they have enslaved are your blood brothers. . . . They must be avenged!

"Come forward to the defense of Christ – make war against the barbarians. You common people who have been miserable sinners, become soldiers of Christ! You nobles, do not feud with one another. Use your arms in a just war! Labor for everlasting reward.

"Let no obstacle turn you aside. Arrange your affairs. Gather supplies. Enter upon the journey to Jerusalem when winter is ended and when spring is here again . . ."

Pope Urban's speech was cut abruptly by a tremendous shout from the crowd. The listeners had been agitated during the last part of his speech and whispering had begun. Finally a single voice cried out, "God wills it!"

"God wills it!" shouted a few more. Men hid their faces. Some began to weep. Instantly all began to shout, "God wills it!" Knights who carried swords raised them high.

"God has drawn this cry from you. Let it be your battle cry. When you go against the enemy, let this shout be raised – 'God wills it!' "

When the speech was finished a huge figure in the middle of the crowd pressed its way forward. It was Adhemar, Bishop of Le Puy. He fell to his knees before the Pope and confessed his sins. The Pope made the sign of the cross. The act of the Pope making the sign of the cross over Bishop Adhemar became known as "taking the cross." Others came forward. Knights, lords, ladies, commoners, and abbots took the cross.

Those who vowed to make the pilgrimage to Jerusalem, by the act of taking the cross, became crusaders sworn to fight until the Moslems were driven from the Holy Land. Those at Clermont were the first members of a band which grew in number to hundreds of thousands. This was to be the holiest and most brutal journey in history.

The Crusading Spirit

The speech of Pope Urban II might seem startling. How could he expect an army of men to leave their homes, possibly forever, to travel three thousand miles on a dangerous journey in the name of religion? Such demands would seem very strange if they were made today, but in Pope Urban's time the call for a religious crusade was reasonable.

At the end of the eleventh century, when Pope Urban sent forth his call to the crusades, loyalty to the Church and to religion was very strong. Nations such as France, Italy, and Germany did not exist. There was only a crazy-quilt pattern of independent dukedoms and baronies. This meant that a knight born in northern France and a tradesman born in southern France might speak the same language but did not belong to the same nation. Each belonged to a small province and to the even smaller feudal estate where he was born. Aside from language, the only thing they were likely to have in common was a devotion to the Church in Rome. The Church was all that held together the Christians in Western Europe.

In fact, many centuries before the call for the crusades, the Church actually controlled what was called the Holy Roman Empire. This empire included all of Western Europe except Germany and Russia; all the lands around the Mediterranean Sea and much of North Africa. This empire did not begin to crumble until barbaric tribes attacked Rome and forced the Roman Emperor to flee eastward to form a new empire at Constantinople in Turkey. This new empire, only a small slice of the old Roman Empire, was known as Byzantium. It spread over Greece, Turkey, Bulgaria, Syria, Lebanon, and Palestine. The shrine of Christ was in Jerusalem. As long as Jerusalem was under the control of the Christian Emperor of Byzantium, it was safe for Roman Christians of Europe to make pilgrimages there.

The Emperor of Byzantium at Constantinople was leader of the Christians of the East. The Pope of the Holy Roman Empire at Rome was religious leader of Western Europe. Everybody believed that a pilgrimage to Jerusalem would purify a person of the sins he had committed. All Christians also believed that the churches and shrines in Jerusalem were especially sacred. To bring back a relic, a chip of stone from a shrine, a jug of water from the Jordan, was to insure God's everlasting protection. This was another strong reason to journey to Jerusalem.

And, many people in the Middle Ages, under the strong

influence of religion, were given to visions — visions that they had seen Christ or a saint, that they were especially chosen to do something extraordinary. Knights and nobles, peasants and tradesmen, lords and ladies — the humble as well as the great — had visions. The Middle Ages was a time when God was uppermost in the minds of men. To be sinful in the eyes of God or the Church was to be lost. Those who made the hazardous journey to Jerusalem were forever respected and honored.

Even as the Holy Roman Empire crumbled and a part of it became Byzantium, it was still not too difficult for the Christians of Western Europe to make the journey to Jerusalem. From France they would go through the passes of the Alps into Italy, cross Bulgaria and travel on to Constantinople, the capital of the Byzantine Empire. From there they took boats across the Bosporus, a narrow strait, to the Asian side. Then they traveled through Turkey to Armenia, along the coast of the Mediterranean to Jerusalem. This route was rough but fairly safe because of the friendliness of the Byzantine Christians.

The Byzantine Emperor's troops were stationed all along the route. Patrols protected the travelers from highwaymen. Inexpensive inns provided food and shelter.

However, safe pilgrimages for Christians to Jerusalem were not to last forever. Around the year 800, a new religion called Mohammedanism arose in the East. The leader of this religion was Mohammed and the people who worshiped him were Moslems. The Moslems were warlike and wished not only to conquer but to spread their religious beliefs through the Mediterranean world. Once they

gained a foothold they were soon able to sweep across the remains of the old Roman Empire. They even battered the frontiers of the Byzantine Empire until they held Palestine and almost all of Turkey with the exception of a small area around the great capital city of Constantinople.

Yet these Arab Moslems granted Christian pilgrims safe conduct to cross their lands to Jerusalem. However, by the middle of the eleventh century, these Moslems were themselves conquered by a fierce tribe from the east, the Seljuk Turks. The Seljuk Turks outfought the Arab Moslems and overran Jerusalem. Unlike the Moslems, who had granted the Christians privileges, the Seljuk Turks were hostile. It did not take long for stories of insults and attacks upon pilgrims to reach the Pope in Rome.

If Jerusalem was completely cut off and Byzantium fell, all Christendom would be in danger. It was with these frightening thoughts that Pope Urban II made his trip across the Alps into France in the year 1095. He felt that he, and he alone, had the influence and power to arouse Western Europe to the danger that threatened the Christian world. Pope Urban had been born in France and he knew that when he spoke to the people in their own language, the religious loyalty they felt toward him as their religious protector would begin to stir and they would follow his leadership.

The Pope succeeded in arousing the people at the meeting in Clermont. From that crowd which shouted "God wills it!" grew the vast tide of Europeans who were to sweep down to the Mediterranean and crusade for the freedom of Jerusalem.

The Knights Prepare

Besides their religious zeal, the crusaders needed practical military might. Thousands of miles of cruel mountains, deep swamps, and dark forests lay ahead. Hunger and disease threatened. Fierce enemies would lie in ambush to attack them.

The responsibility for guarding and guiding the huge pilgrimage on its hazardous journey was placed on the rugged shoulders of the knight. He was to become the military backbone of the crusading armies. Lords, ladies, bishops, pilgrims, children, were to depend on him.

The knight of the Middle Ages was a formidable warrior. He was full of fire and pride. His father had been a noble or at least a knight. He was in the service of a powerful lord under whose banner he fought — and fight he did, for there was continual warfare among the feudal barons.

The knights were eager to take the cross; they had been prepared since early youth for such an adventure.

The education of a knight usually began when he was about ten. At that age he was taught to ride, handle a light lance and practice with a small sword in the courtyard of his father's castle. By his teens he was usually sent to the castle of a relative or friend to continue his training. Now he learned to handle the full-sized lance and long sword. And he learned the code of chivalry — the manner in which a knight must properly conduct himself. The code required him to be unflinching in courage, courteous to women, and a protector of the weak. He learned, in addition, feudal history, hawking and the elaborate ritual of the hunt and tourney, usually from some grizzled knight too old for combat.

After a few years he would become a squire and take on the duties of personal servant and right-hand man to a knight active in the field. He kept his master's armor oiled and polished. He kept weapons sharp. He cared for the great war horses. His master took him to tournaments and into battle, teaching him all he knew.

When the young squire was deemed worthy, he was given a long and rigorous examination. If he passed, he was dubbed a knight at a great feast to celebrate the event. Relatives and friends presented him with a glittering helmet, a suit of shining chain mail called a hauberk, a shield emblazoned in gold and bright colors with his own coat of arms, a two-edged sword, a lance, and a powerful war horse. He was then the equal of any knight in the land and entitled to all the rights and courtesies due his rank. His knighthood was especially cherished by him because it was a hard-won honor. Unlike a dukedom that a young noble automatically inherited on the death of his father, knighthood could not be inherited. It had to be merited and took many years to earn.

This was the training of the knight who was to fight in the crusades. His military education made him bold, courageous, disciplined. The code of knightly honor made him a courteous gentleman. But his experience in battle and in the lists made him a fearless slayer of his enemies.

The knight, then, was both gentleman and ruthless killer. He was the product of the age in which he lived. It was a cruel age, when men plundered and killed without mercy; in which the knight was the best prepared to defend himself. The common people were far less fortunate. For them feudal society was harsh and cruel.

The lowly peasant of the feudal estate was almost always afraid. He trembled in fear at the anger of the ruling baron who could and often did order an ear cropped off or an eye put out. A besieging army could invade the fief on which he lived and run riot, burning his hut and murdering his wife and children. He was nagged by taxes and the threat of famine hung always in the background.

The feudal merchant too had his troubles. The roads over which he traveled were unbelievably wretched. Highwaymen lurked in the forests to rob him. If he was lucky enough to escape the robbers, he had to pay road taxes to the seneschal of every castle he passed. He lived in constant dread of being robbed, tortured or killed by the baron of his own estate or by the baron's enemies.

The feudal baron, though he lived in splendid magnificence, also lived in constant fear – but a fear different from that of the peasant. He was afraid of treachery by other barons or by his own followers who might be plotting against him. To retaliate, he often ordered beheadings or imprisonment to frighten the plotters into submission. The incessant warfare of the feudal baron kept him deep in debt. He had to pay his retainers. He had to pay ransoms for his captured relatives. He had to rebuild damaged walls, barns, and villeins' huts. Often his orchards and animals were destroyed by his enemies.

The knight who went to battle, the baron who had to protect his castle, and the peasant who was all but helpless to protect himself lived in fear. They all committed ugly deeds to stay alive. All of them found comfort in religion. All of them believed in the Church's promise of life everlasting if they confessed their sins. The surest way to have their sins forgiven was to make a pilgrimage.

When, in the year 1095, bishops and monks rode up and down the countryside spreading the message of the crusade and urging everyone to take the cross, there was good reason for such tremendous response. The crusade to Jerusalem was not just a pilgrimage to a nearby shrine. It meant a chance to have sins forgiven forever, to have exciting adventures, and to be rewarded by a happy, peaceful life in Palestine, a country described as a "land of milk and honey." The barons were ready to lead, their knights and men-at-arms eager to do battle, and the peasants, the common men, gathered, thousands strong, to give weight to the crusade.

Peter the Hermit

Pope Urban II had requested that the crusade begin in the year 1096. He did not expect the crusade to be organized or to get under way before the warm bright days of June. He did not suspect that his inspiring message would inflame so many so quickly. He never dreamed that the first crusading army to leave for Jerusalem would be a huge mob of peasants, with only a sprinkling of knights, and many outlaws and that their leader would be a poor monk wrapped in a tattered robe, who rode on a gray mule, his bare feet dangling.

Peter the Hermit, the monk on the gray mule, had been traveling around the countryside preaching when he heard of Pope Urban's summons. He took the cross immediately and began preaching the crusade to others. He spoke with a fiery tongue and boundless enthusiasm. So greatly was

Peter revered that even the hairs cut from the mule he rode became holy symbols to the people.

Peter preached through northern France and crossed into Germany calling on everyone to leave home and join him. Soon he had a great following. Peasants sold their pigs and cows, loaded their pots and bedding on farm carts and joined the throng. Townspeople sold their possessions or gave them to the Church and said good-bye to their neighbors. Unfortunately, many thieves, highway-

men, and criminals of all sorts also joined the crowd to try to rob and cheat their fellow pilgrims.

Peter's crusade assembled in Germany in early April of 1096. There was little discipline in the brawling mob of twenty thousand. The wiser men began to wonder how such a rabble would be fed and sheltered along the way, how the weak, the women, the numbers of children, would survive the endless mountain trails, the deserts, and the enemy attacks. They felt Peter's crusade was doomed from the beginning.

On April 20, it started its long march. The crusaders had to depend for most of their food on what they could buy or beg along the way so they had to keep moving. Twenty thousand hungry people could strip the surrounding villages and farms of food in a very short time.

Those first crusaders were a strange sight. The ragged

monk, Peter the Hermit, led the column on his gray mule. Behind him a small band of knights clanked along on horseback followed by pack horses, wagons, and carts loaded with tents, food, and other supplies. Then followed the huge disorderly mob, mostly on foot. In good weather on dry roads they might expect to make as much as twenty miles a day, but it was early spring and the roads were rough and muddy.

Still, for a while all went smoothly. The crusaders passed through friendly country and were able to buy food and wine and fodder for the animals. The weather held fine. At the border of Hungary they were met by a band of King Kolomon's officers, who permitted them to pass through Hungarian territory in peace on condition that they did not steal or cause trouble.

The trip through Hungary went peacefully until they reached a city near the Byzantine border. Here a dispute between some of the crusaders and merchants in the city grew into a riot. The hotheaded crusaders attacked the city, plundered it and killed four thousand people.

In great fear of quick punishment by the Hungarian king, the crusaders hastily tore down wooden houses and built rafts with the timber to escape across the river at the border into the Byzantine Empire. Once in Byzantine territory, their lust for spoil again grew out of hand and they pillaged the city of Belgrade and put it to the torch. In spite of this savage attack, they were still treated quite peacefully as they moved farther into Byzantine territory.

When they reached a city called Nish, the crusaders began looting again. The governor of the city immediately called out the imperial troops which attacked the crusading mob and soundly defeated them. The crusaders were scattered. Many were killed and hundreds were taken prisoner and made slaves by the inhabitants as punishment for their lawless behavior.

The remnants of Peter's crusaders gathered at a deserted village. When the last stragglers had arrived they took count and found that a fourth of their number had been lost, that their money chest, baggage, and supplies had been captured and that their food was exhausted. In desperation they scattered into the fields to gather the ripening grain and fruit and dig up vegetables and roots. They also slaughtered all the farmers' pigs, chickens, and cows they could find.

Finally the crusaders straggled into the city of Sofia in Byzantine Bulgaria. They were met by the Imperial troops of Alexius, Emperor of Byzantium and religious protector of Christians of the East. Emperor Alexius' troops were given orders to feed the crusaders, keep discipline and escort them to the capital city of Constantinople. Alexius had decided to forgive the crusaders in spite of their savage behavior in his territory. When at last the straggling mob arrived before Constantinople, Alexius gave Peter money and supplies.

Peter's crusaders did not look much like the army Emperor Alexius had expected. He was afraid, in fact, that once this straggling mob crossed the Bosporus the savage Seljuk Turks would make short work of them. However, it was urgent that they leave Constantinople to continue their journey. Many had already begun breaking into homes in the suburbs and looting, even to stripping the lead from the roofs of the churches.

On the sixth of August the crusaders were ferried across the Bosporus. Alexius had advised them to make camp at a town called Civetot, across the Sea of Marmara from Constantinople. He asked them to wait there quietly for the arrival of the more powerful armies of the other crusaders which would soon be arriving from Europe. In the meantime he promised to keep them supplied with food.

Instead of heeding the Emperor's advice, the crusaders at once sent out raiding parties to loot the nearby villages. Finally they attacked the suburbs of Nicaea, the capital of the Seljuk Turks. They aroused the wrath of the Turks by killing and torturing the inhabitants, most of them Christian Byzantines. By now the mob, greedy for booty, was completely out of hand. Peter couldn't control them, and armed bands raided farther into Turkish territory.

In October the crusaders were alerted by spies who sent word that an army of Turks was approaching. Peter's mob, 20,000 strong, straggled out to meet them in battle. In the nearby hills the poorly trained, bungling crusaders entered a narrow pass and stumbled right into a Turkish ambush. Flight after flight of arrows brought down the horses of the knights who led the crusaders' column. The unhorsed knights engaged the Turks hand-to-hand but were overwhelmed one by one in a fierce battle. The rest of the army panicked and fled back to camp, hotly pursued by Turkish horsemen shrieking revenge. The Turks burst into the disorganized camp and slaughtered everyone they could find. When the attack was over only a few crusaders who had hidden in a tower survived, to be rescued by a fleet which came from Constantinople and drove off the Turks.

This was the end of Peter's crusade. Of his twenty thousand followers, almost all were destroyed. It would take an army with more than faith alone to reach Jerusalem. It would need military skill too.

Constantinople

While Peter the Hermit's crusaders were failing so miserably to reach Jerusalem, French and Italian nobles were eagerly taking the cross and slowly forming their crusading armies — armies very different from the disorderly mob which had followed Peter. These troops were made up of heavily armed knights who were grimly aware of the dangers of the journey. These men not only were inspired by the purpose of the crusade but were skilled in the use of weapons of war. The noblemen who were to lead them were practical military commanders. They did not permit the weak, the old, the unfit, to join their ranks. These noblemen, unlike Peter, had a plan. They would march their armies to Constantinople, consolidate their forces, and from there fight their way through the territory of the Turks to Jerusalem.

It took longer for the noblemen to start on their crusade because they had important affairs to settle. They had to arrange for trusted relatives to look after their lands and castles while they were gone. Many of them sold or pawned parts of their estates to obtain money for the journey. A few great nobles sold everything, prepared to leave Europe forever, with their wives and children, carrying furniture, treasure chests, tents, and the rest of their worldly goods with them in heavy wagons. Jerusalem would become their home.

The first to take to the road was Hugh, Count of Vermandois, the tall and dignified younger son of the late King Henry I of France. He left his Countess to look after his domain and marched into southern Italy with a small army of his own vassals and some knights and men-at-arms of his brother, King Philip.

They tried to cross the Adriatic Sea from Bari to Byzantine territory, but their ships were damaged in a storm which sank some vessels with all hands. Hugh and the rest were saved by Emperor Alexius' troops and sent on to Constantinople. When they arrived he and his men were invited to the palace and were shown the sights of the rich, luxurious city, far more beautiful than any in their native France. They were showered with gifts and put at ease.

Alexius was eager to have all the crusaders' leaders accept him as their liege lord and to agree to return to him all the territory he had lost in Turkey if they succeeded in recapturing it from the Turks. In return he was prepared to help them with money, troops, and food in their expedition to free Palestine from the Turks. He was happy to

have them try to establish a Christian kingdom there, because it would be a buffer between Byzantium and Egypt.

The noble Hugh, Count of Vermandois, was awe-struck by the magnificence of the Byzantine court. Alexius saw from Hugh's expression that he would fall easily into his scheme. Hugh had been completely overwhelmed by the splendor of his reception, by the chests of money given him, and by the picture of Alexius himself as he sat on his throne clad in his purple robes. Alexius went to great pains to see that Hugh swore his allegiance, in the belief that those nobles who followed would do the same. It was not long before Hugh took the oath, swearing to devote his body to the Emperor's service.

The next great noble to reach Constantinople was Godfrey of Bouillon, Duke of Lower Lorraine. With Godfrey were his brothers Eustace and Baldwin. The large army of crusaders under Godfrey's leadership was well armed and powerful.

Godfrey had decided to take the overland route as had Peter the Hermit. Without mishap, his army crossed Hungary and Bulgaria. As they neared Constantinople, however, the army got out of hand. Raiding and looting broke out. Emperor Alexius immediately sent envoys urging Godfrey to restore discipline and to march to the city. After eight days of disorder, the officers regained control and the men were marched to a field outside the city walls where they made camp.

Alexius at once sent Godfrey chests of money and presented him with precious jewels. He gave great feasts in the crusaders' honor. Finally he requested Godfrey's allegiance. Godfrey was a proud noble, suspicious of Alexius. He was also aware of the power of the great crusading army behind him. Godfrey sent word that he wanted his army sheltered in the city of Constantinople but Alexius would not consent. The Emperor of the Byzantines did not want the crusaders inside or even around the walls of his city. Alexius pleaded with Godfrey to take his troops across the Bosporus to join the other crusaders but Godfrey refused. He refused also to swear his allegiance.

The situation became ominous. Byzantine military police were posted around the crusaders to watch them, and Alexius stopped sending them food. When the knights went out foraging there were many clashes with these police. The knights finally attacked them in force, and put a number of Byzantines to death. Alexius then lost patience and ordered his bowmen to kill off the horses of the stubborn crusaders. When Godfrey saw the slaughter of his chargers, he knew he had to come to terms with Alexius.

Godfrey deliberated several days and then sent word that he would enter the city alone if hostages were sent to his camp. This was agreed to at once and Alexius promised food and passage across the Bosporus if Godfrey took the oath of allegiance. Godfrey finally was satisfied with the terms and swore by the cross he wore that he would serve Alexius in the coming war. Having come to an agreement with Godfrey, Alexius swiftly made arrangements to have the crusaders ferried across the Bosporus. He wanted to get Godfrey out of the way because he had news that another column of crusaders, from southern Italy, was nearing the frontier.

The army of Bohemond of Taranto reached Constantinople in safety shortly after the departure of Godfrey. Bohemond's army was smaller than Godfrey's but very well armed and trained. On arrival, Bohemond went at once to Alexius and was received with honor. He made no objection to taking the oath of allegiance and swore his loyalty to Alexius immediately.

However, Bohemond, red-haired and with eyes like a hawk's, was an ambitious man. He suggested that Alexius make him commander in chief of all the crusaders including the Byzantine troops Alexius was sending along. But Alexius, fearful of trusting a western knight with so much power, craftily put him off with the promise that when Bohemond had earned command of all the forces, he would be put at their head. In the meantime, Alexius said he planned to send one of his generals with a column of Byzantine troops to join forces with the crusaders.

Bohemond's army was then ferried across the Bosporus. He joined Godfrey, whose camp had grown much larger with the arrival of several bands of crusaders under the leadership of lesser nobles.

On that same day, the 26th of April, another great crusading leader arrived in Constantinople. Count Raymond IV of Toulouse, also known as the Count of Saint-Gilles, a rich and powerful noble, headed a strong army which had marched overland down the Adriatic coast and across northern Greece. They had had a rough time, battling the local Montenegrin and Albanian tribesmen and living on very short rations.

In Thrace where Raymond left them and hurried ahead to Constantinople, they began raiding and pillaging the countryside. At last a Byzantine army had to interfere and Raymond's men were soundly beaten in a sharp skirmish and lost their baggage and arms.

Meanwhile Raymond, accompanied by Bishop Adhemar, was received by Alexius. Raymond felt he should be the military commander of the crusade, and for a while refused to swear fealty to the Emperor. At last Adhemar and some of the other leaders persuaded him to swear a limited oath of allegiance which satisfied Alexius, and Raymond assembled his battered, weaponless army and crossed over into Asia two days after Bohemond.

There was one more army still to come. It set out from northern France in October 1096, led by three great nobles, Robert, Duke of Normandy, his brother-in-law, Stephen, Count of Blois, and his cousin Robert II, Count of Flanders. They crossed the Alps into Italy, where Robert of Normandy and Stephen decided to winter, while Robert of Flanders pushed on with his men to Constantinople. In the spring the first two set out once more and arrived at the capital in May, to join the main army.

At last the crusaders were ready to give battle to the Turks and advance upon the Holy Land. Alexius had managed to get them safely past his capital and now he was ready to help them with men, supplies, and guides, as long as his own empire was not put in danger.

Nicaea

Nobody knows exactly how large the crusading armies were. Peter the Hermit's force was about 20,000, most of them now dead or scattered. Raymond, Godfrey, and Bohemond each headed well-trained armies of about 10,000, including non-fighting men, and there were several smaller armies besides. Altogether, between sixty and a hundred thousand crusaders had crossed the Byzantine Empire in 1096 and 1097.

These rough-mannered, half-savage people from the crude castles and the fields and tangled forests of France and Germany were amazed and dazzled by the great luxurious city of Constantinople. Never had they seen such riches and soft living. Even though they pretended to scorn the wonderful foods and wines, the rich fabrics, the perfumes and jewels, they couldn't help being impressed.

Although the Easterners and the Westerners didn't like or trust each other very much, at least they were allies.

Now the crusaders were to come against a different breed of men. These were the fierce Seljuk Turks, whose country they had to cross on the way to the Holy Land.

The first objective was the strong walled city of Nicaea. It was only a few miles south of the scene of the ambush of Peter the Hermit's army. Nicaea was the capital of Kilij Arslan, Turkish sultan of the region, who was called the Red Lion. Just then the Red Lion and his army were at the other end of his province and the garrison was weak. However, its great double walls, built by the Romans and topped by more than a hundred towers, made it an easily defended fortress. One side faced a lake, with the walls rising out of the water. Without boats the crusaders could not attack there at all.

The men of the Cross surrounded the city and began filling in the moat at several places. Engineers battered at the walls with great rocks cast by the pedreros, or siege engines, and hacked at the base of a tower with picks and shovels under the shelter of a "tortoise" – a great movable shed with a strong roof. The tower finally fell one evening, but before morning the Turks had built it up again.

While the Christian army was vainly trying to breach the walls, the Sultan had been hurrying by forced marches to relieve the city. One hot May morning the crusaders' sentinels sounded the alarm. Down from the wooded hills streamed lines of dark-faced, green-turbaned horsemen, brandishing short curved swords and uttering shrill calls to Allah to aid them. They were the same deadly cavalry

which had so easily routed the knights and men-at-arms of Peter the Hermit's army. Now they surged confidently forward, expecting another easy victory.

These crusaders were far different men from Peter's rabble. Without stopping to put on armor they grabbed swords and lances, vaulted onto the bare backs of their horses and galloped out to meet the foe. The tall, yellow-haired knights astride their great broad-backed chargers crashed headlong into the lighter Turkish cavalry, driving great holes in their line.

But the Turks were great warriors too. More Moslem riders filled the gaps and counterattacked. All day the battle raged; time after time the surprised Turkish cavalry was driven back.

By nightfall the Red Lion realized that the crusaders were too strong. Reluctantly he ordered his horsemen to retreat to the mountains. The city was to be left to its own fate. After dark the Red Lion sent messengers to the city ordering the commander to make the best terms he could with the crusaders. He could give no further aid.

Though the walls of Nicaea were still unbreached, defeat was only a matter of time. The commander of the city knew that when he surrendered, he had better give up to the Byzantine fighters rather than to the crusaders. He would get better treatment from them than from the bloodthirsty men of the Cross. He decided to make a secret offer of surrender to Alexius, who was only too glad to give the Turks the generous terms they wanted — the escape of their leaders.

The crusaders had promised the return to Alexius of all of his former empire. Nicaea had been a part of that empire. Alexius was fearful lest the crusaders take the city, loot it, burn it, and probably kill many of the citizens who were his own Christian subjects. When the surrender terms were agreed upon, the Turks, during the dark of night, softly opened the water gates in the wall fronting the lake. The Byzantine troops of Alexius who had been secretly waiting in boats stealthily crept through the gates into the city. Alexius had outwitted the crusaders.

At dawn of the following morning, when the knights

arose to make ready for an assault, they saw Byzantine banners whipping from the towers of Nicaea. They were dumfounded. They had dreamed of rich loot awaiting them within the walls. Now they saw the Turkish defenders of the city march safely from behind those walls under a truce arranged by Alexius. The wife and children of the hated Red Lion himself were among those who made their escape. What a ransom they would have brought!

Alexius was too wise to leave the crusaders angry and unrewarded. He saw to it that every man got presents, and the leaders shared the gold and jewels found in the Turks' treasury. On the whole, the Christians were satisfied with the results of their first bout with the Moslems, and Alexius was delighted to have Nicaea undamaged, once more under his own banner.

The Knights and the Turks

The crusaders lay in camp for a few days resting and repairing the damages of the battle with the Red Lion's cavalry. Those of the wounded who couldn't travel were sent into Nicaea to recover and help garrison the city. Carts and wagons were reloaded with food and fodder for the animals, and soon the army was ready to go.

The commanders held council to decide on their route, and to work out new tactics against the Moslem troops. The knights from the West found that they could learn a great deal from the Turkish fighting men. During a truce a western knight and a Turkish noble compared their swords. The knight placed a small anvil on the ground and with one stroke of his mighty two-edged sword split it in two. The Turk smiled and plucked a long black hair from his beard and let it float gently down upon his sword blade, which sliced it neatly in two as it touched.

This illustrated the difference between the fighting methods of East and West. The crusaders were bigger, heavier men than the Turks. They wore ponderous steel helmets and their hauberks were made of much heavier links than the Turks', from whom western armorers had first learned how to make chain mail. The knightly sword was a heavy blade nearly six feet long, and lance, mace, and battle-ax were also massive, as was the great war shield. So much weight needed a big, strong horse to carry it, so the crusaders' war horses were as big as modern truck horses, and as slow. The western knights relied on sheer weight and power to roll back the enemy line, by unhorsing their opponents and beating them to the earth with mighty strokes of sword or mace.

The Turks depended upon speed and agility. Their men were smaller than the crusaders, their armor was lighter, because their armorers knew how to make lighter, stronger links of better steel. Their light, wonderfully tempered Damascus blades which would spring back after being bent double were easier to handle and very deadly. Finally, their swift little Arab horses could run rings around the ponderous western stallions.

There were other differences too. Western archers fought on foot, retreating behind the knights' line when the enemy approached. Moslem archers were mounted. They could gallop up, loose a stinging volley of arrows and swoop away, ready for another attack. These archers were particularly deadly against the crusaders' massive charge, because their arrows were aimed to disable the war horses. A dismounted knight was almost helpless against swift Turkish cavalry.

The Turks soon discovered they were no match in a man-to-man collision, so they would attempt to dodge the ponderous charge of the knights, wheel and attack from behind, trying to separate and break up the crusaders' line. The western leaders were learning, too. Whenever they could they attacked the Moslem cavalry at places where they couldn't spread out, because in mass charges they knew they would always win. They learned to keep together, presenting an unbroken line, and they soon made cavalry of their own bowmen, whose crossbows outranged the small Turkish longbow. They began wearing lighter armor under hooded white capes, both because of the fast-moving Turkish horsemen and because of the terrible heat of Asia, where the sun could heat steel armor until it was too hot to touch.

The Christian knights were to learn many other things besides military arts from the Moslems. Generally the eastern culture was much higher than Europe's. Turkish scholars and doctors were much more advanced, and their dyers, weavers, goldsmiths, and armorers made better and more beautiful products than did the artisans of the West. Many of the things brought back by the crusaders became models for western workers to copy.

At last the crusaders were ready to take up the march to the Holy Land. The route led generally southeast across what is now modern Turkey, into Syria, where the great fortress-city of Antioch lay across the path to Jerusalem.

Perhaps fifty miles south of Nicaea was the town of Dorylaeum. To avoid confusion and make it easier to supply the troops, it was decided to split the army into two sections, about a day's march apart. The first was to be commanded by Bohemond and the second by Raymond. On the evening of June 30th Bohemond's division made camp outside Dorylaeum. Tents were set up, horses, cattle, and sheep were watered and fed, and the smoke of hundreds of cooking fires rose into the darkening sky.

Meanwhile, Sultan Kilij Arslan, the Red Lion, eager to avenge his defeat at Nicaea, had been gathering a new army of his own men and those of an ally. Now they were lying in wait, hidden in a small valley, ready to swoop down on the crusaders. At dawn they poured out of the valley in great hordes, shrilling their "*Allah il Allah*" battle cry as they plunged toward the Christian encampment.

Bohemond was not caught napping. He was too good a commander not to be prepared for a raid. Wagons and carts formed a ring, inside which unarmed pilgrims and women filled water jars for the fighters and tended the wounded. Inside the ring, too, the war horses and the flocks were safely tied. The dismounted knights formed a ring around the camp, prepared to defend it against the Turkish horsemen.

The battle began with an attack by the mounted archers. Flight after flight of deadly arrows whistled into the Christian lines, too many finding their mark. Things began to look dark for the heavily outnumbered crusaders, so Bohemond sent swift messengers back to Raymond urging him to hurry.

At midday, just as the Turks were about to overwhelm Bohemond's camp, the troops of Raymond came over the hills. They threw themselves upon the astonished Turks, who thought they had been fighting the whole crusader army. The Moslems were thrown into confusion by this blow from a new quarter. And the rout was complete when a third crusader force under Bishop Adhemar attacked them from the rear. They broke and ran.

The crusaders pursued so savagely that the Moslems abandoned their own camp and fled into the hills. Their tents, supplies, and treasure, a tremendous pile of booty, fell to the knights. Thus in his two battles with the men of the West the Sultan had lost his capital city, Nicaea, and now his camp and treasure. He was too discouraged to try again. His men stripped and burned all the villages along the crusaders' route to keep them from aiding the invaders. Then they retreated far into the mountains, no longer a threat to the Christians.

It was a great victory, but the fighting had been fierce and both Christians and Turks lost heavily in killed and wounded. Women and children as well as priests and monks had been sabered to death by some of the Moslem sallies which broke into the camp, and many knights and men-at-arms lay dead or wounded. The crusaders stayed encamped for several days while the dead were buried and the wounded were bandaged and rested, and more supplies caught up with the army.

The Great Fortress

Finally the expedition moved out again, ever southward, on the road to Antioch. At first their spirits were high. Gay bands of mounted knights and their ladies left the column and rode off over the hills with packs of hunting dogs and hooded falcons, to try to stir up game or birds for sport to add a little zest to their dull meals. Even the constant danger of being ambushed by some wandering band of Turks couldn't keep the crusaders from straying from the column for sport or just sightseeing.

After all, as in all wars, fighting took up only a tiny part of their time. Most of it was spent in keeping alive and as comfortable as possible. Horses had to be fed, curried and watered, and the animals' lame legs and saddle galls needed constant doctoring. Of course they had no refrigeration or canned food, so their meat supply trotted along with them. The pigs, sheep, and cattle had to be fed and watered too.

There was always much sickness, because in medieval times nobody knew enough about sanitation to keep himself or his food and water clean. It was very bad luck to be sick or wounded in those times. Medieval doctors knew very little about medicine or germs. They had a few herbs and balms that sometimes helped, and they could set a simple fracture or saw off an arm or leg, but after that their patients got well or didn't mostly by their own efforts. Most of the badly wounded or very sick died quickly.

The smiths and carpenters of the column were always busy. Weapons and armor needed repairs; bowmen were constantly making, sharpening and feathering arrows and restringing their bows, and the supply carts needed repairs on their wheels and shafts. The women had plenty of work too, making and repairing sandals and clothes and sewing up the rents in their tattered tents.

The greatest worry was food. They were passing through country which was either desert or had been stripped bare. For many years, since the Byzantines had been driven out by the Turks, the land had been fought over so many times that most houses and barns had been burned, orchards cut down and fields made barren. So little remained for the foragers that the army depended mostly on the supply trains from Constantinople.

As the column straggled southward it entered even worse country, a salt desert in which not even a blade of grass grew. Fodder for the animals grew scarcer and scarcer. Some of the horses dropped in harness, too weak to pull the carts. The drivers harnessed cattle and even pigs to draw them. So many war horses died that noble knights had to ride gaunt, bony cows or donkeys.

To make matters worse, the road finally crawled through rocky mountain passes along the sides of steep cliffs where the path was often washed out. Many of the pack animals fell to their deaths and carts broke down forever. The crusaders themselves began to drop, until, by the time they had staggered out of this wilderness, more men had been lost than the Turks had killed in battle.

At last they descended from the wild wind-swept ridges into a land of small villages where they were greeted by ragged, dark-skinned shepherds who held up silver crosses hanging from chains around their necks, to show that they too were Christians. They were Armenians, who had been conquered by the Turks, and they were overjoyed to have the crusaders drive out their hated Turkish masters. To show their friendship they brought in grain, fruit, and fat sheep to the famished Christians, and offered to guide them along their way.

Out of the mountains and desert at last, the crusaders sat down to rest and gain strength for the coming ordeal. Only a short distance ahead lay Antioch, built in the year 300 B.C., once the greatest city in Asia, and during the Roman Empire the third city in the world. It was defended by the Turkish governor, Yagi-sian, who was already feverishly putting his fortress city in shape for a siege. He called in all his troops from the country around, and sent out messengers to the powerful Moslem emirs to the east to send armies to humble this Christian horde.

On the 21st of October, the vanguard of the crusaders under Bohemond swept down out of the hills and halted, spellbound, on the plain before the city. It was an amazing sight. Across the river rose a massive 30-foot wall which ran for two miles along the stream bank. Then it turned sharply and ran along the hills to a mountain ridge. There it turned and followed the ridge for several miles, then turned again and descended to the river, enclosing three great hills, the city, and many orchards and gardens. The wall was so thick that four horses could trot abreast along its top. Four hundred towers, each sixty feet high, were spaced along it. From these, archers could cover every inch of the wall. Five gates, flanked by defending towers, gave entry to the lower city, near the river. They were the St. Paul's Gate on the east, leading to the road to Aleppo;

the Gate of Dogs, opening toward the river; the Bridge Gate, leading to a solitary bridge over the Orontes River, and the Gate of St. George to the west. This last opened on the road to the port city of St. Simeon, on the Mediterranean twenty miles away.

On the highest hill inside the walls stood the frowning, massive citadel, the strong point of the city. Antioch was almost impregnable. The Turks had wrested it from the Byzantines twenty years before, but by treachery, not by direct assault. Could the crusaders storm those walls?

Count Raymond wanted to attack at once, but the other leaders were afraid the battlements would be too hard to crack without siege engines. They finally decided to wait for reinforcements and siege machines which would be coming by ship from Constantinople. Another fleet was rumored to be on the way from Genoa, in Italy. This city had promised the Pope to send troops to help the crusaders. An immediate attack might have succeeded. Yagi-sian was still unready and he might have surrendered. The delay gave him confidence. Besides, he now learned that the Emir of Aleppo was coming to his aid with a large army.

The crusaders were beginning to run short of supplies again. At first they found plenty of food in the nearby villages but soon this was all eaten up and they had to forage farther and farther away. Their foraging parties were continually harassed by Moslem raiders who slipped out of small gates in the walls up in the hills.

A council was hastily called, and it was decided that Bohemond would lead a large force up the Orontes valley to raid for badly needed provisions. As soon as Yagi-sian learned of Bohemond's departure he sent a strong force out of the Bridge Gate and over the bridge to attack the Christians left in camp. At first the surprised crusaders, huddled in their ragged, wet tents pitched in the muddy plain, were driven back in disorder. Then Count Raymond rallied a spearhead of his knights and hit the Turks so hard that they were driven back across the bridge and through the open gate. Just as it looked as though the knights might gain a foothold inside, a riderless horse plunged onto the crowded bridge. The men-at-arms, confused in the darkness, fell back, and the Turks were able to close the gate and bar it.

Meanwhile Bohemond's seven hundred knights, mounted on all the horses left in camp fit to bear them, trotted up the valley. That night they made camp, but

Bohemond kept the men alert. Guards were posted, scouts sent out, and the horse lines well watched. His caution paid off, because at daybreak his scouts returned to report thousands of horsemen approaching. It was the army of the Emir of Aleppo, swordsmen and mounted archers, ready to attack only seven hundred knights mounted on hunger-weakened chargers. The knights had not a single man-at-arms or bowman to support them. Only the ground was in their favor. The lakes protected one flank and the swamps the other so that the Turkish cavalry couldn't outflank them.

The crusaders waited. They had to, because their sick, bony horses were not up to a long, hard gallop. Now the Moslem arrows whispered past. Some struck solid flesh and emptied knightly saddles, but the iron men stood fast, waiting. At last the Turkish line charged, and the knights lowered their long lances and crouched in their tall saddles behind the taut blazoned shields to meet the rush of steel and flesh. They met with a crash and a fierce ringing of blades and the crusaders bored in, only to falter against the weight of the enemy's numbers. Bohemond threw in his last card. His reserves thundered into the melee and crumpled the Turkish first line like paper. The other knights rallied and followed and the great swords rose and fell, biting through the helms and mail of the Turks. Nothing could withstand those terrible iron men and their whirling naked blades. The Turks broke and scattered to their camp, snatched up whatever they could carry, fired their tents and fled.

The crusaders triumphantly pursued them, loaded up

all the treasure and food their weary horses could carry and turned back to their own camp before the walls of Antioch. As they approached in the slanting shadows of late afternoon they saw their own men-at-arms and archers left behind to guard the camp, in a last-ditch action against a powerful force of Turks from the city garrison. Yagi-sian, now seeing the knights approaching loaded down with booty, realized that they must have beaten the Emir's relief army and hastily recalled his men. The beleaguered city would not now be rescued, but Antioch's great walls still protected her. Would the crusaders now stage an assault or lay siege and try to starve out the Turks? These were the questions in Yagi-sian's mind, but he did not guess what would really happen.

The Fall of Antioch

The Christian army now settled down to encircle the city and prevent supplies from getting in or raiding parties from slipping out. They built towers opposite the city gates and soon the Turks were cut off from the outside. More and more ships were arriving from Constantinople and Cyprus at the port of St. Simeon with supplies, siege machines, and fresh troops to fill the thinned ranks of the Christian army.

Merchants and traders began to appear, eager to sell supplies and food to the crusaders. Just as things seemed brighter for the Christian army, native spies reported that the Turkish Sultan Kerbogha was on the march with an enormous army to lift the siege. Discouraged and frightened, many of the crusaders began to slip away and desert. Stephen of Blois turned tail with his soldiers. Even Peter the Hermit tried to desert, but he was brought back.

While many of the crusaders were losing heart Bohemond had been working on a plan. He knew that many Turks might be bribed to turn traitor, and finally managed, through spies, to get in touch with such a man. He was an Armenian officer named Firuz, turned Mohammedan, who was captain of the Tower of the Two Sisters and a section of the main wall. Firuz, with a grudge against his Moslem superiors, would take a bribe, for which he agreed to let the crusaders climb the wall in his section at the right time.

On the very day that Stephen and his men deserted, Firuz sent word to Bohemond to pretend to lead his army eastward late in the afternoon, as if to face Kerbogha's advancing army. As soon as darkness fell they were to return with scaling ladders to the western walls and mount them at his tower, where he would let them in.

Bohemond called a meeting of the other leaders and explained the plan. That afternoon the Turks saw the Christian army streaming away to the eastward, and were fooled into believing they would have a peaceful night.

Just before dawn the crusaders crept softly up to the base of the wall, their feet and ladder tips wrapped in rags, swords and lances held tightly to prevent any clatter. Cautiously a long, limber ladder was raised to a dark window in the tower, and one after another, sixty knights carefully mounted the rungs in pitch-blackness and crawled through the window. Creeping softly along the wall they overcame the guards in the towers on either side of the Two Sisters, so that the troops below could raise their ladders safely along that whole stretch of wall.

A swarm of knights and bowmen clambered over the battlements and down the stairs into the sleeping city to overpower the guards at the St. George Gate and the Bridge Gate and throw them open to the troops waiting outside. Most of the Turkish soldiers, including the Governor, Yagi-sian, fell before the first rush of the crusaders' assault. Native Christians as well as Turks were tortured and killed, their houses looted and destroyed. As the sun sank into the western hills on the third of June, scarcely a Turk remained alive, and the streets were piled high with corpses. Antioch was under the Christian banner.

However, the crusaders still had fighting to do. While the Turkish garrison which had constantly raided their lines was nearly destroyed and they themselves were behind the city's strong walls, there was another problem. Kerbogha's vast army was approaching and the crusaders were far too few to man all the walls of Antioch. In addition, they had to picket the great citadel built into the wall, which still held a Turkish garrison. Further, they soon found that the city's food was very low. The traders who brought in bread, vegetables, and meat asked such high prices that only the wealthy nobles could afford them. After Kerbogha's men surrounded the city, the common soldiers and poor pilgrims even chewed leaves and bark and leather clothes to ease their hunger.

The Sultan tried an assault from the citadel which his troops could enter from outside the wall, but the western knights had built a low wall around the citadel inside the city, and they were able to drive back the Moslems with heavy losses. After this costly repulse, the Turkish commander decided to lay siege and starve out the Christians.

Bohemond and the other crusader leaders pinned their hopes on rescue by a large imperial army which was marching from Constantinople.

But this help was not to come. The Emperor Alexius was met by Stephen of Blois who had deserted from Antioch just before the crusaders captured it. Stephen told Alexius that by now the Christian army must have been completely destroyed and the Turks in control again. The false news caused Alexius to order his army to turn around and march back to defend Constantinople. The victorious Turks might now decide to counterattack the Byzantine capital, they reasoned. When the crusaders heard about his retreat they felt that Alexius had deserted them.

Famine and discouragement brought the Christians' spirits low. Then rumors began to spread through the city that a poor peasant, Peter Bartholomew, had seen the spirit of St. Andrew in a vision. The saint told him to dig under the floor of a certain church where he would find buried the lance which had pierced the side of Jesus Christ. This holy relic would lead them to victory.

Some believed Bartholomew while others thought he was a fake. Arguments and disputes swept through the

town. At last a group of twelve knights were chosen to go to St. Peter's Cathedral with Peter Bartholomew to see if the lance was really there. After many hours of fruitless digging they were about to give up, when Peter himself jumped into the hole and promptly brought up an old rusty lance tip, which he proclaimed to be the sacred lance. Although some skeptics thought he might have planted it himself, a wave of new courage swept over the majority of the crusaders. The leaders decided to risk all in a heavy surprise attack upon the Turkish camp.

Early in the morning of June 28th, all but 200 men left as a garrison were drawn up in six divisions. They were ready to risk all in a desperate thrust against an enemy which far outnumbered them. The gates were unbarred and thrown open and the knights plunged across the bridge into the Turkish camp. The Turkish archers tried in vain to stop the charge; the mighty iron men were soon among the enemy, whirling their swords and maces over their heads and reaping swaths of Moslem cavalry.

As the Moslem line wavered, many of the allied Emirs lost heart and pulled their own men out of the fight, weakening Kerbogha's army. Suddenly panic spread through the Sultan's troops and they began to flee. He had the dry grass in front of his men set afire in a desperate attempt to delay the Christians but they plunged right through the flames and scattered and slaughtered the Turks by the hundreds. Soon the Sultan's army was no more.

The crusaders turned back at last to loot the Turkish camp and returned triumphantly through the River Gate, loaded with spoils and now complete masters of Antioch.

On to Jerusalem

Now that the enemy had been destroyed the crusaders had time to think of their own jealousies and feuds. The northern French disliked the Provencals from the south, and the Normans from Italy distrusted both. Many of the smaller nobles wanted to establish kingdoms and duchies of their own, while the two great leaders, Bohemond and Raymond, were bitterly jealous of each other. Bohemond felt that since he had planned and executed the capture of Antioch, the city should be given to him. Raymond, who was on good terms with the Emperor Alexius, felt that the crusaders should be true to their oaths and return the city to the Emperor Alexius.

Many of the nobles scattered, raiding for loot and for cities to rule. Those in the city took things easy now that plenty of food and wine was coming in.

In July a terrible sickness broke out in Antioch and hundreds died of it. Many of the leaders hastily moved out of the city. They encamped in villages and towns in the country until the epidemic, which was probably typhoid fever, died down. During this plague, the crusade suffered a tragic loss. Bishop Adhemar, the wise and well-loved leader, was struck down by the fever and died. The loss of his counsel would be sorely missed during the months to come.

While the crusaders quarreled among themselves at Antioch, the Fatamids, rulers of Egypt, saw their chance. The defeat of Kerbogha by the crusaders had so weakened the fighting power of the Turks that the Shah-in-shah, al-Afdal, grand vizier to the boy Caliph of Egypt, al-Mustali, decided to invade Palestine. His troops besieged the mighty walls of Jerusalem, which was defended by only a very weak garrison. After 40 days of pounding by great stones hurled against the walls by Egyptian siege machines, the defenses were so battered that the Turks surrendered and were given safe conduct to Damascus.

The Egyptians then occupied Palestine as far up the coast as Beirut, a city halfway between Antioch and Jerusalem. This coast was studded with a chain of walled fortress-cities, Latakia, Tortosa, Beirut, Sidon, Tyre, Acre, Haifa, Caesarea, and Jaffa. Some were held by Seljuk Turk garrisons who were now cut off from their Sultan, and the more southern cities by Egyptian troops.

The Turkish garrisons were now eager to surrender to anybody who guaranteed them safe conduct, but the Egyptian forts were another story. Most were built at the edge of the sea, with protected harbors which could be supplied by sea – and the Egyptians had a great fleet of war galleys and many supply ships.

To meet this new enemy, the crusaders had a choice of two routes to the Holy City. They could march along the Orontes River and then southward in the valley east of the coastal mountains and so avoid having to capture all the coastal cities. However, a good part of this route lay through waterless desert country and it would cut them off completely from ships bringing supplies from the Byzantine islands of Cyprus, Rhodes, and Crete. They had been depending on these supplies all along, and were afraid they might be in trouble if they were cut off.

The other route was straight down the coast, where they might have to subdue the walled cities to prevent having their supply line from Antioch cut off by the Turkish garrisons after they had passed.

In addition to choosing a line of march, there was another problem. Bohemond and Raymond each hated to leave the other in control of Antioch, and the days dragged on with no action. At last the troops themselves began to demand that the crusade move on to its goal. Men who had signed on to bring the Cross to the Holy City, wanted to finish the job and go home. Besides, many weeks of feeding thousands of mouths had combed the countryside bare of food.

At last Raymond realized that Bohemond, whose men held Antioch, would never give it up and that he would have to move. On January 13, 1099, his army marched out of Maarat al Numan, a town a few miles south of the city, where he had been encamped. They left the city in flames to prove that they would not return, headed by Raymond walking barefoot as a devout pilgrim should. The crusade had delayed 15 months at Antioch.

For a time, their way led inland where they found the local princes, instead of hostile, very eager to help with food and guides. They marched quickly southward without any fighting. Now they had to decide which road to take. Raymond's army was down to 1,000 knights and 5,000 men-at-arms. With so few men it seemed impossible to conquer all the walled cities ahead. On the other hand, the inland route lay through the country ruled by Emir Duqaq of Damascus, who would certainly fight them every inch of the way. The council decided they would take the coast road.

When they reached the Mediterranean, Raymond sent a small column northward to try to capture Tortosa, the only good harbor along that coast. The force was too weak to storm the walls, so they tried a trick. That night they built a ring of campfires all around the town to make the Turks think they were being besieged by an enormous army. The ruse worked. The Governor of Tortosa was so frightened that he ordered the garrison to abandon the fort by sea that night. In the morning the crusaders marched into an undefended town whose harbor made it possible for Byzantine supply ships to bring in food.

This quick success made the leaders still lingering in Antioch jealous, and soon Godfrey of Bouillon and Robert of Flanders marched down the coast to join Raymond's army. Bohemond came too, but soon returned to his prize,

Antioch. As the crusaders approached Tripoli the Emir made peace and presented them with food and badly needed pack animals. Again without fighting, they were able to cross the Dog River and pass over the Egyptian-held frontier of Palestine, the Holy Land. There were no Fatamid troops so far north and the governors of Beirut, Sidon, and Tyre offered them rich presents and free passage, so they moved so swiftly that they arrived at Ramle, only 30 miles from Jerusalem, on June 3, 1099.

A few days later, at the village of Emmaus, they were met by some of the Christian townspeople of Bethlehem, the birthplace of Jesus. They begged the crusaders to free their village from Moslem rule, so Tancred and Baldwin of Le Bourg took a company of knights and went back with them. When they reached the village the Egyptian troops had fled. The people were overjoyed to see the Cross again, and came out to kiss the crusaders' hands, and put on a procession with all the holy relics from the Church of the Nativity.

Next day, after Tancred's knights rejoined the army, they moved up the road to the summit of the mountain where stood a small mosque of the prophet Samuel. The nobles and knights stood silent, staring across the dusty valley. Before them rose the massive gray walls of a great fortress city. At last the crusaders' eyes beheld the end of their long quest, Jerusalem.

The Siege

For centuries Romans, Byzantines, Turks, and Egyptians had been building and strengthening the walls and towers of Jerusalem until it had become one of the great medieval fortresses. In addition, the Egyptian enemy was alerted well in advance. As soon as the Fatamid governor, Iftikhar ad Dawla, learned that the crusader army was approaching, he began preparing. All Christians living in the city were expelled, because they actually outnumbered the Egyptian soldiers, and, although they were peaceable and bore no arms, they *could* do much damage during an attack.

Iftikhar's men drove all the flocks of sheep and herds of cattle from the surrounding pastures into the city, filled in or poisoned every well or spring and cut down every tree for miles around. The crusaders would find a barren, waterless, timberless land for miles around the city walls.

Storehouses were well filled with food, and though there were no wells or springs within the city the old Roman cisterns were brimming with rain water. The governor sent swift messengers to Cairo to ask for quick reinforcements, and distributed his garrison along the tops of the walls, armed and alert. He had done all he could, the next move was up to the Christian dogs.

As the rising sun reddened the grim battlements of Jerusalem on the morning of June 7, 1099, the crusaders' army spread out over the desolate plain and prepared to besiege the Holy City.

Both the attackers and the garrison had too few men to guard the entire circle of walls around the city. The crusaders left the eastern and southeastern sides unguarded and occupied the sectors where they could get nearest to the walls. Robert of Normandy camped before Herod's Gate, next to the men of Flanders under Robert, who lay before the Damascus Gate. Godfrey of Bouillon took station to the northwest before the Jaffa Gate, along with Tancred. Raymond of Toulouse took his stand to the south, on Mount Sion.

The leaders held a council of war to plan the attack. Already they realized that a long siege was out of the question. The Moslems had ample food, water, and shelter, while the crusaders lay encamped in a barren, foodless, waterless, and shadeless plain in the full heat of the Palestine summer. Except for one small spring within dangerous range of bowmen on the walls, the nearest water was six miles away, and the water carriers could be ambushed by raiders sneaking out of gates on the unguarded sides of the city. Not a tree was left to build siege machines or even ladders. The sun beat down on the unprotected men until their armor was too hot to touch. The stench from carcasses of horses, cattle and sheep killed by hunger and thirst lay like a pall on the camp.

The leaders sought the advice of a holy man, an ancient hermit who lived in a cave on the Mount of Olives. They assembled on June 12th and heard him proclaim that they must attack at dawn on the next day. To their protests that they had no siege machines or ladders he insisted that they needed only one ladder. He said God would lead them to victory if they attacked at dawn.

Many crusaders were doubtful, but a few weak and shaky ladders were patched together, and the army attacked at dawn as the hermit had commanded. After several hours of bloody combat the commanders saw it was hopeless. Either their faith had been too weak or the hermit was a fake.

The princes conferred again on the 15th and decided to delay until they could build siege machines, assault towers, and ladders to mount a proper attack. On the 17th by the greatest good luck a fleet of six Genoese and English ships found Jaffa, the port city for Jerusalem, unguarded by the Egyptian navy, so they sailed in and anchored in its harbor. They were loaded with just what the crusaders needed: bolts, nails, rope, and tools for making siege machines. Quickly pack trains were sent the 20 miles to Jaffa to bring up these precious supplies. They were just in time, because an Egyptian fleet appeared off the harbor as the last boatload was rowed ashore. The Christian sailors had to abandon their ships to escape capture, and join the crusaders on shore. Even then, the column was ambushed by Moslem raiders on the way to the Holy City and was rescued just in time.

The crusaders still needed timbers to build the machines, but there was no wood nearer than the hills of Samaria, fifty miles away. They finally sent working parties there to cut down trees and bring them down on the backs of captured Moslems and camels. Then the engineers of Gaston of Béarn and William Ricou set to work sawing the logs into planks and building mangonels, catapults and ballistae, as well as two great siege towers, one for Godfrey and one for Raymond.

The men labored in the searing heat, their tongues coated with dust, their throats parched. The only water,

foul and muddy, came by camel load in waterskins. It brought enormous prices. Slowly the work continued, but the men were low in spirit and many quarrels broke out. Some even tried to desert to the ships at Jaffa, only to learn that they had been captured by the Egyptians.

Spies brought in dismaying news. A great Egyptian army was on the march from Cairo to break the siege. If it arrived before the city was taken, the Christian army, caught between the garrison and the attackers, was done for.

Just as things looked blackest a priest, Peter Desiderius, reported that the dead Bishop Adhemar had come to him in a vision and revealed that if the crusaders held a three-day fast and then walked barefoot around the city walls, Jerusalem would be theirs within nine days.

Adhemar had always been loved and respected by all the crusaders, so this vision was enough to bring new hope and courage to the troops. The workmen set to with fresh vigor to finish the siege machines. Even the old men and the women helped by sewing hides together to protect the towers from Greek fire, a flaming mixture of tallow, resin, turpentine and crude chemicals which could be hurled from the walls of medieval cities by the defenders. Women also worked at weaving great shields of willow boughs for use against stones and arrows.

Every knight and soldier was filled with fiery determination to do or die, partly because of Desiderius' vision, and partly because the goal for which they had suffered so much for so many months at last lay before them.

All the crusaders fasted for three days as directed in the vision. Then on Friday, July 8th, they formed a long procession. Barefoot all, the long column moved slowly around the city along the path below the walls. Bishops and priests were in the lead, holding high their crosses and holy relics. Behind them came the princes and their knights in full armor, flaunting their bright banners, and followed by the archers and men-at-arms. Last were the pilgrims and the rabble of common men.

The Moslems atop the walls jeered at them as they passed, but the crusaders were too filled with the spirit of their holy undertaking to pay any notice. After they had encircled the city they climbed to the top of the Mount of Olives, where Peter the Hermit and several other priests preached to them. They returned to the camp in high spirits and went at the task of putting the last touches to the siege machines. All was ready for the final assault.

The Great Assault

The leaders decided that the attack would be launched on the night of the 13th of July. One spearhead would drive against the eastern part of the north wall. Another was launched at the same time against the northwest side as a feint. The fighting men in the entire attack numbered twelve to thirteen hundred knights, twelve thousand men-at-arms and archers, plus a large number of armed peasants and pilgrims.

The first goal was to bring the siege towers close enough to the walls for their drawbridges to reach the battlements. All day long the attackers threw stones and fagots into the moat before the towers, to fill it, losing hundreds of sturdy yeomen to the barrage of searing Greek fire, stones and arrows poured down on them from the walls. In reply the Christian siege engineers cranked back the arms of their mangonels and ballistae, pulled the triggers and released them, to hurl great rocks against the top of the walls and flaming fagots into the city itself. Clouds of dust rose from the shattered stones of the walls, and flames shot up from the burning houses. Flights of flaming arrows rose toward the battlements and crossed other flights descending on the heads of the attackers. Above the thud of the great battering rams pounding against the foundations of the walls rose the screams of the wounded.

Files of villeins were rolling great rocks to the siege engines, others carried bundles of arrows to the crossbowmen. Torchbearers stood ready to light the straw-wrapped fire arrows just before they were released.

As the rubble in the moat mounted to ground level, great "sows," or movable sheds on rollers, were pushed slowly forward until they touched the base of the walls. Scores of half-naked villeins, armed with crowbars, picks and shovels, swarmed into them, and began to hack and pry, to try to loosen the great fitted stones of the walls. They were protected by the sturdy roofs of the sows, covered with wetted hides against Greek fire and fire arrows, but an occasional huge rock arching from a siege machine on the parapet crashed through. Then the shrieks and groans of the wounded rose above the din of the attack.

The scorching heat of midday beat down cruelly on the wounded lying on the shadeless plain.

All day the fighting raged. When at last the shadows lengthened and the battle slowed, the walls were still unbreached, but one thing had been accomplished. Godfrey's tall siege tower now stood on its rollers atop the filled moat very close to the walls.

As darkness fell the soldiers ate their meager rations, washed down with warm, foul-smelling water, and wrapped themselves in their cloaks for a few short hours of rest. Along the protecting palisades before the siege machines and in the tower sentries watched tensely, against any sally by the Egyptians. For a time torches flickered in the tent where the commanders planned the next day's assault. Presently all was quiet.

When the first pale light of dawn of the fifteenth of July, 1099, outlined the grim towers and massive battlements encircling the city of Jerusalem, the defenses already bristled with the spears of Egyptian warriors. Below, all along the crusaders' lines, the oliphants, great war horns, blared defiantly against the shrill cries of the Moslem defenders. The knights and men-at-arms of Godfrey of Bouillon, Robert of Normandy, and Robert of Flanders were poised to attack on the north side, from the Damascus Road to the Tower of David. The Provencals prepared to assault from the west, and Count Raymond's men on the south.

The tall siege tower designed by Gaston of Béarn, master siege engineer of the crusaders, was now in position very close to the walls. From its topmost level, protected from enemy fire arrows and Greek fire by freshly wetted cowhides nailed to the tower frame, crossbowmen cranked up their arbalests and began pouring flights of deadly bolts down upon the garrison along the walls. On lower stages of the tower mailed knights waited tensely, their shining steel helms pressed down over the hoods of their chain-link hauberks, or mailed shirts. With their great

crested battle shields on their left arms and naked long swords in their right hands, they were ready to spring forward the moment the drawbridge of the tower crashed down upon the battlements.

Behind and below, the air was full of the sound of straining timbers and creaking ropes, as the heavy wooden arms of the massive siege engines were bent back, then suddenly released to hurl huge stones, heavy darts, and flaming missiles up onto the crowded battlements.

This morning Gaston of Béarn had brought all his ballistae, mangonels and catapults for a mass attack at this point. Under cover of their fire several "cats," huge battering rams suspended by chains from wheeled frames, were pushed against the gates to begin pounding at them. The ram men were protected from arrows and fire from the walls by sows.

Just out of range of Moslem arrows stood many teams of laddermen, ready to raise their scaling ladders against the walls at the right moment. Behind them, armed with axes, lances, pikes, and swords, the rank and file of men-at-arms, in steel caps and heavy leather jerkins, were drawn up, prepared to mount the ladders.

Protected by a barrage of missiles and arrows, teams of the strongest yeomen now put their shoulders to the siege tower. Slowly and shakily the ponderous structure crawled ever nearer to the massive walls.

During the night the Egyptians had labored to repair the crumbling walls and increase their height with wooden barricades. These barricades had bundles of straw piled against them to give shelter from the deadly crossbows on the tower. Behind the barricades the Egyptians had lined up extra catapults and mangonels which now opened a blazing barrage of stones, arrows, burning fagots, jars of Greek fire and burning oil against the crusaders. The men in the tower fought desperately, rewetting the hides to save it from the flames. The success of the attack hung on protecting the tower.

Just in time the Christian bowmen were ordered to loose a volley of arrows wrapped in blazing oil-soaked cotton into the straw of the barricades. In a moment the battlements were a roaring sheet of flame, driving the defenders back.

In the confusion two knights leaped from a hastily raised scaling ladder to the top of the wall and managed to keep a desperate foothold. At once more ladders crashed against the wall and men-at-arms swarmed up over the battlements to throw themselves into a hand-to-hand struggle with the Moslem defenders.

This was the critical moment. Godfrey roared a command to cut the ropes holding up the tower drawbridge. As it crashed down upon the wall a wave of steel-clad knights wearing the crimson cross on their shoulder dashed across it shouting the crusaders' battle cry, "God wills it!" Their long flashing blades cut down the Egyptians on all sides and soon drove them in panic down the stairways into the city streets.

The knights plunged after them, swept the guards from the gates and opened them to the waiting troops outside. Soon the maddened crusaders were driving Moslems, Jews, and even native Christians through the narrow

streets, into the houses and onto rooftops and slaughtering them by the thousands. Jerusalem had fallen!

Now, for the first time in four hundred and sixty years armed Christians were able to walk freely through the streets of the Holy City.

Jerusalem

Jerusalem was won for the Cross. Terrible and senseless destruction gutted the city in the madness of the first few days. Raiding, looting, slaughtering of Moslem and native Christian alike went on. There was total disorder. This was the usual pattern of conquest in medieval times.

Meanwhile, a ruler had to be chosen for Palestine. The noble chosen would be the first Christian to rule Jerusalem for more than four centuries.

There were four great nobles to choose from, four leaders who had started on the great journey and who had survived the battles to reach the holy city. Who would it be? Godfrey of Bouillon, Raymond of Toulouse, Robert of Flanders, or Robert of Normandy?

At first Raymond was asked to take the crown, but he knew that most of the crusaders did not really want him, so quite wisely he refused. Godfrey was then chosen. He was well liked by all. Godfrey felt that since Jerusalem was the holiest place in all Christendom it ought to be ruled by the Church. However, there was no church leader in the Holy Land great enough to accept the responsibility. Because of this, Godfrey agreed to rule but he refused to be called king. His title was Baron of Jerusalem and Defender of the Holy Sepulcher.

Godfrey's first responsibility was to meet the threat of the Egyptian army that was marching up the coast from Cairo to attack the crusaders. Godfrey decided it would be wiser to meet the Egyptians in the field. He assembled a force of disciplined knights. Once more the crusaders would do battle together.

In a swift march down the coast, Godfrey's force soon came upon the Egyptians. By good fortune they found them asleep and unprepared. Their commander had never expected to be attacked so soon. It was a brutal battle. Though the knights were outnumbered, surprise and discipline helped them defeat and destroy most of the enemy. Those who were not killed fled in disorder. The crusaders captured immense booty. But that was not the most important part of the victory. Egypt's power was broken and Jerusalem was safe.

Godfrey ruled for only a few months. He fell ill with typhoid fever and after lingering for a few weeks he died. He was buried a hero. His brother, Baldwin, took his place as ruler. Baldwin was a forceful, able leader who soon conquered all the small cities and castles around Jerusalem. Egyptians and Turks fled the countryside and the crusaders settled down to what they thought would be a long period of peace. Some thought the Holy City would remain forever in Christian hands after the First Crusade, but that was not to be. For the next four hundred years there were seven more crusades. A new age of great wars was just beginning.

The crusaders had captured Jerusalem but that is not all the story. When peace was restored to the city — peace which was to last a hundred and forty-five years until the Second Crusade — knights, squires, pilgrims, bishops, and great nobles longed to go home. They wanted to see Europe again. They were lonely for their families. They left the holy city, some retracing the route they had traveled during the crusade and others returning by sea.

The crusaders who decided to leave had been gone for as long as three years. They had seen many strange sights and learned much during their great journey. They took back not only the story of those three years but knowledge of the arts and crafts of the people they had conquered.

Their distrusted allies, the Byzantines, the hated Turks and the Egyptians were far ahead of Europe in arts and crafts. At the time of the crusades Europe was only beginning to rise out of a dark and savage period in her history. The crusaders performed a deed of great importance when they brought back the culture of the East.

Not only was there transfer of knowledge from East to West, there was also a flow of gold. The commerce that resulted from the shipping of food, arms, and equipment to the crusaders in Jerusalem brought wealth to many merchants, artisans, and farmers in Europe. Cities like

Genoa and Venice in Italy and Marseilles in France became rich trading ports.

For a time Christians and Moslems lived together in harmony, but the Moslems would never be content so long as the intruder from the West was in their midst. In time the Turks would recapture their lost provinces and the crusaders would again be forced to leave their European homes and march to the East to do battle with them.

The Crusades Continue

In the year 1144, the Turks captured a province near Antioch called Edessa which had been taken from them by the Christians. As in the First Crusade, when the people of Jerusalem called to Pope Urban II for help, the people of Edessa, in 1144, appealed to Pope Eugene III. The threat of the Turks to Christendom by the capture of Edessa inspired the Second Crusade.

The purpose of the Second Crusade was not to make a great journey to Jerusalem but simply to retake Edessa from the Turks. The leaders of the new crusade were Conrad III, Emperor of Germany, and Louis VII, King of France. These great nobles led their armies into the land of the Turks but were routed, leaving Edessa in the hands of the enemy. Those who escaped went to Jerusalem to settle or returned to Europe. There was not another crusade for fifty years.

During those fifty years, the Turks steadily hacked away at the borders of Palestine. In 1187, a great Moslem leader named Saladin led his armies to a victory in which Jerusalem fell to him. This started a new wave of crusading fever which resulted in the Third Crusade. This crusade was led by three great kings, Frederick Barbarossa of Germany, Philip Augustus of France, and Richard the Lionhearted of England.

Its purpose was to recapture Jerusalem for the Cross and was very much like the First Crusade in spirit. All Europe was again astir with feverish preparations. Even women took the cross. Swedes and Danes put to sea to help. The whole continent was up in arms.

The armies of the three great kings met before Acre in the holy land and captured the city after a fierce battle in 1191. However, jealousy among them grew and soon the Germans and French withdrew. This left the army of Richard the Lionhearted to fight alone. The English fought bravely and well but did not have the manpower to take Jerusalem. When he saw he could never capture the city by force of arms, Richard signed a treaty with Saladin, which allowed the Christians to hold the Mediterranean coast between Jaffa and Tyre and gave them the right to visit the Holy Sepulcher at Jerusalem unmolested.

The Fourth Crusade came a few years after the treaty with Saladin. It was organized in the year 1202 by Pope Innocent III and was led by a great noble of Venice, Boniface, Count of Montferrat. Instead of making an attack on the Turks at Jerusalem, Boniface attacked the city of Constantinople. The crusaders sacked the city, dethroned the Byzantine Emperor and set up a new western Emperor. Boniface marched no farther east, never even crossing the Bosporus to fight the Turks.

Nearly twenty years had elapsed since the Third Crusade had departed from Europe with such gallantry. Its brilliant silk pennants fluttered and the sunshine flashed from the polished armor of the brave knights in the trains of the three great kings, Frederick, Philip, and Richard. They had returned weather-beaten and ragged, their mission a failure. The Moslems still flaunted their banners over the most sacred shrines of Christendom.

People were ashamed and discouraged. No great leader had risen to lead them on another gallant expedition against the Turks. Every year a day of mourning was set aside, when the crosses were draped in black and the people prayed for a great leader to head another crusade.

The Children's Crusade

One day, a small shepherd boy of twelve sat on a stone in the fields watching his flock of sheep. Perhaps he was dreaming of the day when he would be old enough to join a new crusade himself. Stephen's father was a poor shepherd who lived with his family in a humble hut in the tiny village of Troyes. None of the family had been more than a few miles from home. None could even read.

Suddenly a mysterious, cloaked stranger appeared, sat beside Stephen and began to talk to him. He said he was an old crusader, with a mission for Stephen. God, he said, had ordained that Stephen was to lead a crusade of children to the Holy Land. Armed knights had failed to free it by force of arms. Now, with God's help, a band of innocent children would convert the infidel, not with weapons but because they were pure of heart. Then the stranger gave Stephen a letter to the King. It directed him to help Stephen gather an army of children to carry out his sacred task.

The boy was full of zeal for his new work. Everywhere he went he told of visions which had come to him, proving that God was with him. People in those days were only too ready to believe in miracles; the children especially were overjoyed to think that one of them had been chosen to lead a crusade. Many of them flocked to Stephen and to other boy leaders who claimed to have had visions too.

These young leaders formed processions which marched through the countryside singing hymns and shouting the crusaders' old battle cry, "God wills it!" Everywhere more children joined and took the cross. Parents who tried to lock their children up to keep them from joining such a foolhardy undertaking found that they broke out and left without a backward glance. Those who couldn't escape pined away until they had to be released, then they also followed the bands. Of course many children joined for the excitement and adventure, or to get away from hard jobs and daily chores, but some really were carried away by religious feeling.

Not only children joined. Priests and monks, servants of rich children, who were sent to look after them, and parents of some of the youngsters also took the cross. But others besides good people came too. Criminals, thieves, and the scum of the city slums flocked to this crusade, looking for easy pickings.

By now nothing could stop the movement. Stephen sent word through France that the children were to gather at Vendome, early in the summer, ready to start. By this time the excitement had spread all over Europe. In Cologne lived a boy named Nicholas, who had heard about Stephen and wanted to lead a crusade of his own. He also had visions and instructions from on High. He was eager to tell about them to any who would listen.

Soon the crowds of German children were gathering just as they had in France, until by June, 1212, Nicholas and his aides (there must have been some adults along to advise this twelve-year-old boy) decided to move.

Outside the city, encamped in the fields and under the trees, was a vast crowd of 20,000 boys and girls, monks and priests, good people and criminals, all awaiting the signal. Here and there were groups of parents, the fathers grim, mothers sobbing. They were making a last desperate plea for sons or daughters to give up this crazy, perilous scheme and come home.

The youngsters were from all walks of life. Some of them were children of poor peasants who had never been more than ten miles from home. They had not the slightest idea of where or how far away Jerusalem was. Some were children of noble birth who had lost relatives in the

Fourth Crusade. Many of these were supplied with horses and had servants, money and food.

All the young crusaders knew of their destination was that they must march south until they came to the shores of the great sea. When they reached it their leaders told them the waters would open magically before them and let them walk dry-shod to the Holy Land.

At last the trumpets blew a fanfare, and Nicholas and his escort took the lead. The bands of crusading children, mostly boys of about twelve years, fell into line, singing and waving their banners and crosses. At first they traveled through friendly country, among people who spoke their language. The weather was good, villagers generously supplied them with bread, cheese, and fruit, and sometimes even milk. They slept under trees and hedges at night. It was like a big, gorgeous picnic.

All too soon the thieves and criminals began their dark and bloody work. Children with money, jewelry, or food were robbed. Sometimes their clothes and shoes were taken too. Even worse, local barons and burghers from the towns along the way kidnaped many of the strong, healthy-looking boys and girls and forced them to become slaves or servants for the rest of their lives.

When they reached Switzerland their route lay through wild, heavily forested country with very few houses. There were only a few very bad roads, and these were infested with bandits.

Now before the children lay the great snow-capped ranges of the Alps, barring their way to Italy. These were the first mountains most of them had ever seen. There were no roads, only steep, narrow trails that clung to the sides of cliffs, sometimes disappearing altogether where slides had wiped them out. Only a few rickety bridges spanned the roaring mountain torrents. Mostly, the rivers had to be waded at fords. Over these dangerous trails the children toiled, half-starved now, chilled and worn out. Every night many died from cold and exhaustion. During

the day many more fell over cliffs or were drowned fording the swift icy streams.

By the time the column reached the pass at the summit of Mount Cenis, less than half of them remained alive. The astonished monks who kept the monastery there to aid travelers were filled with pity at the wretched condition of the children who were still alive. They gave them shelter, food, and medicine for a day or two while they rested. The monks tried to persuade them to give up, but next morning they started bravely down the trail into Italy. From each rise they looked hopefully for the blue sea.

The Italian villages along the road still remembered the cruelties they had suffered from Barbarossa's German crusaders. In revenge they treated these German children badly. By the time the children looked down and saw the beautiful Bay of Genoa spread out below them, they were a miserable lot, their spirits almost broken.

It was Saturday, August 25, 1212, when Nicholas's band limped up to the gates of Genoa. The boy sent a message to the Genoese senate. He begged permission for his crusaders to spend the night in the city and be given food and shelter. They would remain only one night because, on the morrow, the sea would open a dry path for them to the Holy Land.

The Genoese opened their gates and the bands of children swept in. It was the largest and most beautiful city most of them had ever seen. They stood openmouthed before the great marble palaces, the statues, the busy shops, and the great harbor teeming with shipping. They were fed, and as night fell some were taken into houses. The rest slept in doorways and under bridges.

As dawn brightened, even the sleepiest child hurried down to the shore. Now they would see the miracle of the dividing waters! They stood silently in thousands watching the sparkling waves—and watched and watched. Nothing happened; hour by hour they waited, until slowly the terrible realization came that they had been tricked. There would be no magic road to Jerusalem.

The children were brokenhearted. They were ragged and penniless, hundreds of miles from home in an unfriendly country. By now Nicholas, their leader, had disappeared and they had no one to advise them. Some decided to stay in the wonderful city of Genoa and try to make a living somehow. Others turned their faces homeward, and still others thought they should walk farther east. Perhaps they had come to the wrong place for the magic path through the sea. These reached Pisa, and had no better luck there. The remnants of the crusade got to Rome, where the Pope told them to go home and grow up. Then would be time enough to fulfill their vows to retake the Holy Land. So ended Nicholas's Crusade.

Another column, which was too late to join Nicholas at Cologne, left Germany a little later, and crossed the Alps at Saint Gotthard. Afterward they marched down the length of Italy as far as the town of Brindisi, down in the toe of the peninsula. They suffered much the same hardship and cruelty as did the first column. They were also foiled by the sea's failure to open. Many died or were enslaved and only a few managed to straggle home.

Back in France, Stephen's Crusade got a later start. By

the end of July, though, they were 30,000 strong.

Stephen, the once-modest twelve-year-old shepherd, had his head turned by all the attention. As the column started, he rode at its head in a beautiful chariot with a silken canopy overhead. He was attended by a troop of youths of noble blood mounted on prancing chargers and armed with swords and lances.

Their road lay entirely through France, among their own countrymen, who treated them kindly. There were no harsh, snow-capped mountains or wild forests across their path; the country was well settled and so they had less trouble finding food. Thus they were able to travel the 300 miles to Marseilles and the Mediterranean faster than the German column.

The 30,000 children swarmed into Marseilles and waited impatiently for the morning, when the sea would open for them. The troubled citizens looked at them sadly, shaking their heads. They had lived here beside the sea all their lives and they were far from convinced that the miracle would come to pass tomorrow.

The Mediterranean was no kinder to Stephen's Crusade. The vast waters still tumbled and tossed all through the day, as they had for thousands of years. The townspeople were worried over the future of these thousands of youngsters now. What would become of them? Some urged them to turn back and go home, and many finally did, but just then something wonderful happened.

Two merchants of the town, who said that their hearts had been touched by the noble aims of the crusade, offered free passage to the Holy Land to 5,000 of the children.

Everybody rejoiced at the generosity of the merchants. Thousands of the young crusaders volunteered.

The merchants had seven ships rigged, watered and victualed for the voyage; each would hold about 700 children. On sailing day the whole town was at the waterfront to wish the children Godspeed. It was a solemn and beautiful occasion. Groups of priests and monks were assembled on the high poops of the ships, chanting hymns of rejoicing. Sometimes the high, clear voices of the children crowded on the main decks below joined in. Bright banners fluttered above them and the sun winked from the burnished crosses.

As the tide turned fair, the captains ordered the sails loosed and the anchors raised. As the chains rose dripping from the bottom, the ships started gliding slowly away from the docks. Then as the sails were sheeted in, they moved more swiftly out into the harbor. Cheers rose from the crowds ashore, answered by the singing from the ships, until the vessels cleared the harbor mouth and set their courses for the Holy Land.

Then months passed without a word from the little fleet. Returning pilgrims and sea captains were questioned anxiously, but nobody had seen or heard of the flotilla. Months passed into years, and at last even the most hopeful gave up. Then, in 1230, eighteen years after the crusade had vanished, an old priest arrived in Marseilles with the first news. One of the crusade's passengers, he told a terrible tale of disaster and treachery.

The little fleet had sailed with fair winds and sunny skies, southeastward for three hundred miles. Then, as they passed along the western coast of Sardinia, a great storm broke. Those early ships were clumsy and hard to handle, almost helpless in a gale. They sailed very badly into the wind. The sailors watched helplessly as the gale drove them ever nearer the coast. Off Sardinia a small island, San Pietro, lay ahead a little to leeward. If only they could clear it they would have plenty of sea room to ride out the storm.

Ever nearer they were driven to the cruel rocky shores, pounded by enormous breakers. Five of the ships, those farthest to windward, managed to claw their way clear of the deadly rocks, but the two nearest were blown helplessly toward the wild surf. Those on the other ships watched with sinking hearts. Suddenly the two hulls were seized by the great breakers and flung against the reefs.

In an instant they were smashed to bits against the sharp rocks. For a few moments a few black dots were seen struggling in the white foam, then a succeeding breaker swept in and nothing remained alive on San Pietro.

The five remaining ships weathered the storm and sailed on, their passengers saddened by the tragedy. All unknowing they themselves were soon to be victims of a worse fate. The young crusaders knew nothing of geography or navigation or they would have become suspicious of their course. The ships were no longer sailing east toward the Holy Land, but southwest.

Soon a dim blue coastline appeared ahead, and from it came scudding a fleet of swift black war galleys. As they approached, the monks and the children were horrified to see the crescent banners of the Moslems streaming from

the mastheads. They had been betrayed by those kindly Marseilles merchants. Instead of giving them free passage to Palestine, these terrible men had sold them into slavery to the Moslems.

The French ships put into the harbor of Bujerah, in Africa. Swiftly the children were driven ashore and handed over to slave dealers, who carried them off to Egypt, Damascus, and Baghdad. Some of them saw Jerusalem on their way to their new homes, but they saw it in chains. Not one of them ever saw his home again.

One hundred thousand children took part in the Children's Crusade. One third of them never returned to their homes. In eight months over thirty thousand children perished, were enslaved or lost. For many years thousands of homes all over Europe mourned sons and daughters lost in the Children's Crusade.

After the Children's Crusade there were three more crusades to Jerusalem. These last three crusades were fought by armies of knights and nobles against the Turks. Each failed. In fact, by the time of the Eighth Crusade, the final one, in 1291, every inch of territory that had been taken by the Christians of the First Crusade had been won back by the Turks.

The crusades could only have happened in a feudal land, where nobles, knights, and priests held absolute power. Yet they were so deeply religious that they were ready to sacrifice their lands, wealth, and even their own bodies to follow the Cross.

After Pope Urban's call to arms, for almost two hundred years armies of Christian crusaders swept across Europe into Palestine to do battle with the Moslem hordes out of the plains of Central Asia. For a few years they were successful in building and holding a Christian kingdom around Jerusalem, only to see it fall to the conquering Turks. By 1453, the Turks even took mighty Constantinople, the capital of the great Byzantine Empire, and drove out the last Christian from Asia Minor.

Although the Holy Land was lost, the crusades were not entirely a failure. With so many of the quarrelsome, hotheaded nobles and knights away, the kings of western Europe could at last put their domains in order. Now they could bring the castles of their powerful nobles under a central government. This marked the beginning of separate nations speaking a common language with a central government. They replaced loose-knit groups of dukedoms, each in constant warfare.

In the Holy Land the crusading nobles learned to get along with each other against their common enemy, the Moslem, and so were able to live together more peaceably when they returned home.

Europe was just beginning to emerge from the ignorance and crudeness of the Dark Ages. For two centuries the crusaders had been exposed to the higher culture of the Moslems, and had lived in houses, eaten food and worn clothing made far better than any they had ever known in the West. As soldiers they soon found that Moslem steel and workmanship produced arms and armor far superior to their own, and that Arab physicians cured their wounds and fevers more skillfully than western doctors could. Thus, over the years the crusaders brought back more and more Moslem ideas, crafts, and skills, which hastened Europe's climb from the depths of the Dark Ages.

Index